# The Human Spirit

## An Example

**A story of survival and kindness in Russia, 1939-1945**

**As told by David and Genia Krimalowsky**

Translated, transcribed and edited by Peya Carmi Robinson

**In memory of Sherah Liat Robinson**

**Dedicated to**

**Helah Liza Robinson**

**Asaf Anshel Lang**

**Gil Avraham Lang**

## Introduction

When my father, David Krimalowsky, fled from Poland at the beginning of the Nazi invasion in 1939, he carried with him a journal tucked away in a small waterproof leather bag. This little bag was attached to his belt and never left his sight.

For five years he kept a journal, documenting his journey to and experiences in Russia.

My mother, Genia Krimalowsky, had a little bag of her own, where she kept money she was saving to bring home to Poland to help her mother and her sister.

After the war, my parents found out that their respective families were murdered by the Nazis at Auschwitz.

On their way to Israel moving through unfriendly countries my parents had to destroy family pictures and important documents. They never understood why this was necessary—it was merely an order from the person leading them. Among the documents destroyed was the precious journal.

Once in Israel, birth certificates and other documents could be acquired from Poland, and pictures were copied from originals owned by my uncle, who had left Poland long before the war. But the journal was lost forever.

My sister Shoshy and I grew up listening to stories about the past, told mainly by my mother.

Eventually, when my dad was over eighty years old, he decided to tell about his experiences in Russia so his grandchildren would have some knowledge about him, his wife and their life at that time.

He wrote from memory, sometimes recalling the information he wrote in his journal, sometimes reconstructing stories as much as he could.

When I read his writings and had questions about dates, names and descriptions, he was already forgetful and sometimes I couldn't get clear answers. Therefore, I had to fill some gaps of information with the knowledge I had from listening to my parents' tales when I was little.

We'll have to accept it as it is told here. David's stories are displayed in regular font, Genia's stories are displayed in italicized font.

This is for you, Helah, Asaf and Gil. I hope you enjoy and appreciate these stories and will be proud of your grandparents.

I love you,

Peya

Moscow
Belarus
Poland
Russia
Warsaw
Łódź
Rozhysche
Czechoslovakia
Ukraine
Slovakia
Hungary
Romania
0
50
100
150 miles

## Łódź, Poland

September, 1939

On the evening of September 1, 1939, at a time when the days were tense, and the nights were filled with anxiety, my partner guard and I were sitting during our night shift listening to the radio. [Editor's note: David never specified what he was guarding and why, but our assumption is that news of the impending Nazi invasion had reached the town, and there was a general alert.]

Suddenly there was an announcement: "All men of enlistment age must flee the city."

I went immediately to the police to get more information and instructions. When I entered the station it was empty. Everybody had left. Forms, documents and papers of all sorts were spread on the floors and even outside in the street.

When I returned to the post my girlfriend Genia was waiting for me. She had been sent by her brothers to tell me they were waiting for me at their home so we could leave Łódź together.

I left for Genia's home to discuss the logistics of departure with her brothers. I planned to then go home to get ready and say goodbye to my family. Upon my arrival, however, I discovered that Genia's brothers hadn't waited for me and had left already. Without a second thought, I followed them.

On September 1st 1939 I left Łódź with a map of Poland and ten Zloties in my pocket.

I never saw my family again.

## The Escape

The Polish army was withdrawing to Brzeziny [a village approximately 24 km west of Lodz, Poland] and we followed them. Anti-aircraft artillery posted along the escape route shot at the German airplanes that were strafing the people on the ground. In an effort to dodge German bullets, people were running along the road and then diving to hide in the potato fields. When the airplanes finally disappeared, heads began popping up through the foliage, looking around to see if the coast was clear. I can still remember a heart breaking scene when a man's screams pierced the silence. He was yelling "Haim, Haim!" but Haim didn't answer. He never would. The man continued to yell and cry for a few more minutes and then stopped. His voice follows me to this very day.

Soon people were back on the road, running by foot, riding on wagons and bikes, and in cars. "The runners," or *"der loifers"* as we were called in Yiddish, were fleeing in complete chaos, but all in one direction—to Brzeziny where the Polish army was headed. Along the way, we were going to stop in the smaller city of Zomkowetsye. However, as we approached I could see billowing smoke rising from the town and knew it was already burning. I was fortunate enough to have brought a map with me, which showed a side road that curved right and avoided the city and led instead to a little town called Góra Kalwaria. [34 km south of Warsaw]

Three men in front of me were driving a wagon loaded with old certificates, documents and other archives and had been refusing to let anyone ride with them. I showed them the map and explained my plan to bypass Zomkowetsye, hoping they would give me a ride because my feet were blistering and my energy was waning. They followed my directions and about fifteen kilometers later we came to train rails leading to Góra Kalwaria.

We continued along that path and soon came across a road sign pointing towards Warsaw. People began arguing over which direction we should go. Some believed that because everybody else was going to Warsaw, we should do the same. I, however, thought Warsaw would be the worst place to end up for two reasons. First, the very fact that so many people were going to the capitol would inevitably lead to a food shortage. Second, the Germans could declare victory only after the capitol has surrendered, and would therefore bomb Warsaw the most. After much discussion, everyone agreed with me and we turned away from Warsaw.

We rode for a while and arrived at a bridge over the Wistla (Vistula) River where some units of the Polish army were crossing. Because they had priority, we were not allowed to cross so we camped for the night and slept.

In the morning we were told about a shallow point of the river where there would be no danger in crossing by foot. We rode along the riverbank and sure enough, we found the crossing spot.

We all undressed, rolled our clothes around our shoes and put them on our heads. We walked in the water on both sides of the wagon. When the wagon tilted to one side, the people on that side caught it and straightened it.

When we arrived at the other side, we thought the danger was over. We thought we were free.

That was not the case. As soon as we got dressed, we noticed the runners again, only this time they were joined by soldiers.

Order emerged out of chaos. If a car stopped and blocked the road (damaged or out of gas), people immediately gathered together, pushed the car off the road to enable the runners to advance.

Once in a while the flow was interrupted. A thirteen year old boy was riding his bike, behind him was an officer riding his horse. The officer knew, sooner or later, the horse would collapse. He shouted towards the boy, "Lets trade." The boy, knowing it was a bad idea, shook his head, and in a flash the officer jumped off his horse and yelled to the boy to give him the bike. The boy stuck his toes into the bikes wheels crying: "Nye dum". (I won't give!). The officer yelled and beat the boy. This continued for a while, until the officer gave up.

The horse, meanwhile, went to graze in the field.

All that time, nobody said a word, let alone interfere.

Why?

I assume because it happened at an abnormal time. And at a time like that there is no 'Why?'.

The runners used to run in twos or threes. Very seldom one person was seen running alone. The routine was the same—when we heard airplanes, we spread in the fields and hid. When the airplanes disappeared, we came out. Not everybody reappeared.

Scared of being robbed, farmers and villagers tried to keep the runners from entering their homes.

When we approached their houses, the doors and windows were closed with signs on them, announcing, "Boyek Typhus" which meant "There is Typhus here".

Sometimes, a farmer felt sorry for the starving, tired refugees and "let" a chicken or a duck "escape", so the runners could eat.

When we got a chicken or a duck, we cut off their heads and then covered the bodies with clay. We started a fire, put the clay-covered bird in it. When a smell of roasted foul floated around, we broke the clay. The feathers had stuck to the clay and when it was stripped off we had a clean roasted chicken or duck.

Shoes presented a big problem. Many people walked barefoot and whoever owned shoes had to guard them closely, since stealing shoes was common. We usually slept with our shoes under our heads.

The sleeping problem was as bad.

We would get thrown out of one barn, only to be thrown out of another one, until finally the farmers got tired of yelling at us and we got a restful night.

Due to shortage of food and guards, the government released prisoners. They were recognized by their shaven heads.

When shaven heads appeared, they created a serious problem for us, the "runners".

We wanted only to pass the night somewhere but the shaven heads would steal whatever they could and the farmers would become strict again. Eventually the farmers had to guard their animals themselves and when they saw that we were not the "shaven heads" they would occasionally allow us to sleep in their barns.

One day when we came out of a barn we saw an airplane overhead. It was a Russian airplane which meant we had made it to Russian controlled land. We leapt for joy and many were weeping.

We were not happy for long. The Poles where returning to Poland, and on their way they were shooting Jews who were running the other way to Russia.

So we had to travel at night, to avoid the Poles who traveled in daylight. Eventually, only Jews were seen on the roads.

Finally, we arrived at the outskirts of a town named Rozhysche, in the Ukraine, on the border with Poland. We were afraid to enter since we heard gunfire, but as more and more people arrived eventually we had to enter the town.

My escape and run from Łódź to Rozhysche lasted about twelve days.

## Rozhysche

Upon entering the town, I went to a nearby creek, washed myself and cleaned my clothes. I laid my clothes on stones in the sun, and after they had dried, I got dressed and went into town.

While walking along an alley, a hand stretched reached out and grabbed my shoulder pulling me into a depression in a wall. Before I realized what happened, a voice yelled at me: "Don't you hear the shooting? You could have been killed!"

My savior was the "shamash" of the town. (Shamash: a person who assists in the operation of a synagogue and acts as an assistant to the rabbi). His name was Berger, a joyful man, who had a wife and a child.

My first lodging in Rozhysche was at the home of Mr. Berger.

On Friday night (Shabbat eve) Mr. Berger took me to the public bath. His wife gave me a bar of soap, and clean underwear. She also wanted me to hand over my dirty ones. I told her I could wash them myself. "I know how you can wash them. I saw you in the creek." she said. I gave her my dirty underwear without another word.

I didn't understand Russian, and was always asking "Kakoy?" ("What?") and that became my new name. When Mr. Berger introduced me to the committee in charge of refugees' affairs he said, "Here is a guy who knows everything." I introduced myself as David Kakoy, and that was my name until I left Ukraine.

During my stay Rozhysche hosted a national choir contest for the Ukraine. I was called to a meeting where we were given a list of popular songs of the era.

I met with the Commissar and suggested to build background scenery for the popular song, "The Three Tankers". He approved of my idea and I got all the materials, equipment and manpower I needed.

Choirs came from all over Ukraine to participate in the contest. One choir, composed of three male singers, attracted special attention due to one of its members who had an incredible bass voice. The floors shook when he sang. He was even better than the famous bass in the synagogue choir of Łódź, who was known as "Meir Bass."

The three men choir received first award. My group came in second.

I was in charge of the food stamps given to the refugees. One day [~Jan 1940] I recognized one of my friends from Łódź, standing in line. At the end of the day we got together and exchanged information. He and his friend just arrived from occupied Poland and knew how bad the situation was. They planned to go back and save their families.

I got fired up at the idea—this was my opportunity to do the same. We agreed to meet the next morning, after I retrieved my belongings from Mr. Berger's house.

The next morning the two friends came up with a different idea. Since my position in town was very important due to my access to food, they argued that it would better serve everybody if I stayed in town and they would go on the trip. They promised to save anybody I asked for. Mr. Berger agreed with them.

After a short argument I gave in.

I stayed in town and the two of them took off.

The Jews in Rozhysche welcomed us with open arms. I still remember the rolls and meat they provided for us.

But the continuing stream of refugees created a shortage in food and living quarters and people had to stand for hours in line to get food. Help appeared in a form of a Jew farmer named Dov Torchenuke from a neighboring village. He offered to find accommodations and food for a few dozen Jews. I was one of the lucky ones.

The refugees were distributed among the Jews in the village. I was assigned to the home of Dov's father in law, Reb Moshe Oxman, a proud and wealthy Jew.

The neighbors filled me in how Dov became his son in law.

Dov, a Yeshiva graduate and a certified Rabbi, had also been a rebel in the Czars' time and had to flee Russia.

He found refuge in Reb Oxman's estate where he earned his living by teaching the Oxmans' children. He fell in love with one of his students, Oxman's oldest daughter, Henia.

She was 13 at that time and he waited five years until he could marry her. Although Reb Oxman didn't approve (he did not want his daughter to marry a poor rebel), they got married.

I arrived at the village on the high holy days. I was blessed to attend a public prayer I'll never forget. Dov prayed in front of the congregation all day long. He also read the verses from the Torah. He had a very deep, impressive voice. His prayers and singing touched every heart.

I became a permanent guest in Henia's and Dov's house. They had four pretty daughters who lived with them (Shoshana, Hadassa, Pnina and Shula), and a fifth, Bat-Zion, who lived in Israel.

Torchenuke's home was grand and noble, infused with culture and very Zionist. They had shelves of religious and secular books, magazines, and newspapers in Hebrew, Yiddish and Russian. This was quite a amazing thing to find in a small Ukrainian village. It was a warm and welcoming home.

Dov was a scholar and a wonderful conversationalist. We spent hours playing chess and debating on different subjects, sometimes way into the night.

The family loved to sing, especially Pnina. And so, in spite of the worry about the future and the sadness in our hearts, songs flooded into the night through the open windows, into the wide fields.

## ***Genia's tale of the departure from Łódź***

*I stayed in Łódź and the Nazis entered the city.*

*First thing they burnt a synagogue and hung a few Jews.*

*I had to wear a yellow star on my blouse, in front and on the back.*

*Germans that were Polish citizens became men of authority. They were brutal and mean—they scared the Jews and enslaved them.*

*For example, one night a Polish German entered our apartment. The windows were covered due to the black out. He looked around and shouted: "Are you spies?" We knew he came to check if there was anything of value he could steal and had hidden everything valuable ahead of time. When he realized there was nothing to take, he left.*

*Another time I was summoned with a few other girls to a German Polish man's home. He ordered us to clean. Every once in a while he released a girl or two. Finally, we were only three girls. We got worried that he would demand more than just cleaning. Suddenly a few Nazis arrived. He was scared of them as much as Poles and Jews were scared of them, so he forgot about us and we slipped away.*

*When David's friends arrived with their offer to take with them whoever wanted to join, my mom, my sister and I didn't know what to do. My mom was too old to travel. She knew she would become a burden and Ruza, my sister, refused to leave her behind. Both couldn't decide if it was safe to let me, the "baby", join strangers, and travel in an unfriendly country to an unknown destination.*

*We went from one neighbor to another seeking advice. Everyone had the same thing to say: "I wish somebody offered to take my child".*

*David's mom and his sisters decided not to go.*

*His older sister, Lea, just got married and moved to her own place. His younger sister, Ruza refused to leave her old mother alone.*

*On departure day, my mom couldn't stop crying. I kept ensuring her repeatedly "Don't cry mom, I'll be home in no time."*

*The future was unknown, but I preferred to leave so there would be one less mouth to feed.*

*Tsesha, the girlfriend of one of my brothers, joined the departing group.*

*I never saw my mother or my sister again.*

## A Rude Awakening on the Way to Russia

The Russians and Germans had signed the Ribbentrop-Molotov Pact, also called the Nazi-Soviet Non-Aggression Pact, in late August of 1939.

We were told that every person volunteering to work in Russia would have his family released from Poland. Of course we volunteered by the dozens to go to Russia, with the hope of seeing our families free in Ukraine.

We went to the nearby city, Rovna, in Ukraine to shower and get immunized.

All the volunteers were concentrated into the cars at the end of the train. Looking back, I understand it was designed to make sure we couldn't change our minds.

On that day, Genia and Tsesha arrived. They ran from one train car to another but we were too far away. They didn't find us. The train started to move and we were leaving Rozhysche, on our way to Russia.

Our eyes shone. Every small hut looked to us like a big house. Every big house was a factory in our eyes. We accepted everything with a lot of enthusiasm.

On the border between Russia and Ukraine we had to change trains because the train rails in Russia were twelve and a half centimeters wider than those of Ukraine. Passengers from Russia had to transfer to Ukraine trains and vice versa. On the platform I met a friend's brother.

"Were are you going?" he asked.

"To Russia" I said.

"Well, I have been to Russia and am on my way back." said the fellow.

"What happened?"

"Nothing happened, the revolution hasn't happened yet. The red army is killing communists!"

I boarded the train, continuing to Russia, perplexed.

Our I.D. cards were taken away. That was like cold water on my enthusiasm. Everybody knew that without an I.D. card you are as good as a prisoner.

While riding on the train I made a decision to survive. I knew I could rely only on myself, and my contrivances.

My talents, quick thinking and inventive imagination helped me survive as a refugee in communist Russia during World War II.

## Genia's story from the road

*Our group advanced during the nights. During the days we found hiding places.*

*Most of the Poles were anti-Semites. Only money stopped them from murdering us or giving us away.*

*Once we took refuge with a Polish family who we paid in advance. When we got ready to leave, one of the older sons blocked the front door and asked for more money. He threatened to get the Germans.*

*I tried to appeal to his heart, telling him we were poor people and gave him as much as we could. He took my hands in his and said: "These are not hands of a poor working- woman. They are soft and delicate!" We had to pay more money, which was very much needed later.*

*An interesting episode happened to us when we had to cross the Wistla (Vistula) River. It was the beginning of winter. The river was half frozen. This was the most dangerous time for crossing the river. Only experienced guides knew how to find frozen spots to cross safely.*

*The refugees hired guides to lead them across the river. When we arrived at the riverbank we could see candles lights flickering on the surface, held by guides leading escaping refugees.*

*Sometimes we heard screams. That meant a guide had misjudged the ice, and his group fell into the water, usually freezing to death.*

*We asked a leader of a group that was ready to move if we could join for a fee. He left his group, and led us across the river.*

*I don't remember if the other group followed. I was probably too frightened to notice.*

*Tsesha and I arrived in Rozhysche on the same day when David and my brother left to Russia.*

*The Berger family took us into their home.*

*Henia Torchinuke heard about the arrival of David's girlfriend and sent me money, claiming David left it for me. She gave me money a few more times.*

*David, of course, had no money to leave for me. Henia did this out of kindness.*

## A factory in Communist Russia

We came to a leather processing factory located next to the town Abzesche. We were assigned collective living quarters, men separated from women. Rows of beds, with a closet between every two beds, were lined up along the walls. We were given money to buy food and necessary supplies.

Then we were gathered in a large hall to listen to a welcome speech. The speech was very nice—we were told that if we worked like loyal Russians we would become loyal Russian citizens and at the end we applauded.

The next morning we got our work assignments. I was to be the apprentice of a pregnant woman who prepared leather for ironing. She was throwing up very often and when she felt the need she just turned her face away, threw up and continued to work. No break.

We were standing on both sides of a table, loaded with leather pieces. At our feet stood buckets containing some oily liquid (leather softener), and rags. The woman soaked the rag in the oily liquid, brushed a leather piece and then, with two oily hands, grabbed the leather and transferred it to the ironing machine.

I followed her example but I didn't like the procedure. Our hands were oily and the grip on the leather was not steady. We were in constant danger of the leather slipping and falling taking us with it.

That night I lay awake in bed images of my childhood floated into my mind. In my neighborhood we had a bakery located in a basement and on cold winter days when we couldn't play outside, we would gather next to the front door of the bakery to watch the baker and tell stories.

Then I recalled a Friday morning when the baker prepared Challas for Shabbat. He dipped a brush in a beaten egg yolk and brushed every Challa before baking. After baking, the Challas had a nice shiny gloss.

An idea popped in my head.

Next day I collected sacks, sticks and ropes. After work I prepared a brush from two sacks, two sticks and a rope.

I took the brush with me to work and used it to dip in the oily liquid, brushing the leather without getting my hands oily. With dry hands I transferred the leather to the ironing machine.

The foreman was walking through the aisles, checking the progress of the new workers. He inquired about my progress. My trainer said "Look, no oily hands, no danger. This fellow found a solution".

In the center of the hall hung a bell that was rung when important news was to be delivered. He rang the bell, everybody gathered around us. He described my idea to improve efficiency in the factory and gave me a reward of thirty eight Rubles, a very nice sum in those days.

He called me to his office and asked me to look around and find more ideas for improvements. I didn't need convincing—the money was important.

Everywhere in the factory there were signs imploring us to improve productivity. I opened my eyes, starting thinking, and opportunities followed.

One of the steps in processing was drying the leather which took place in an extremely hot room. When I arrived at the factory only Gypsies worked in that room. They had to hang the leather pieces to dry on sticks and then separate them from the sticks in the hot room. The room was never cooled.

The drying process was as follows:

A. The leather was hung to dry on sticks over a pit.

B. When the leather had dried, someone would hit the sticks and they would fall into the pit with the leather pieces attached to them.

C. A worker entered the hot pit, separated the leather from the sticks and threw the sticks out for re-use.

D. The leather was loaded on wagons and carried away.

The main hardship was separating the leather from the sticks. The heat in the pit caused the leather to stick very hard to the sticks, and it took a long time to separate them. Shifts in the pit were long and miserable. The gypsies wore only long under shirts and when they came out of the pit a stream of sweat followed them on the ground. Finally they couldn't stand the conditions and simply left.

Nobody wanted the gypsies' job so it was decided that everyone would have to take part in this dreadful process. Each of us was assigned a two-hour shift working in the pit.

When my turn came I stood next to the opening and looked at the sticks and the leather. The foreman walked by and said "You have to do your part—start working."

"Looking around is also working." I replied.

Knowing me, he didn't push.

After a while I came up with an idea to avoid having to enter the pit. Instead of knocking the sticks into the pit from above, I grabbed each stick, pulled it towards me, and the leather fell into the pit ready to be loaded. The stick was still in my hand, and I merely set it aside for re-use.

In five minutes my job was finished and I saved myself two hours of discomfort. I sat down and rested.

An hour and a half later, the foreman came by to check on my progress. He was very upset.

" Why aren't you inside, doing your job?" he asked frowning.

"I finished my quota." I answered and showed him the leather waiting to be loaded.

The bell was rung again. My contribution to the "Efficiency of Production" was announced and again I got a monetary reward.

Now, I became known and respected—two important facts that helped me get my I.D. card back, and with it my freedom.

In the middle of 1940, about six months after my arrival the engineer in charge, a Jew, invited me to his office.

He asked me for some help. The factory was changing the measuring method from weight in kilograms to length by foot, probably due to export requirements. He asked me to design and produce stamps, for imprinting the measurements on the leather.

Those were days of war and he couldn't trust Moscow to supply new stamps on time.

I argued that I had no knowledge or experience in this kind of thing, but he was insistent so I took on the task. I received a signed form giving me the permission to get whatever I asked for.

The shoemaker gave me rubber, the carpenter supplied the frames and I got to work. I fit the rubber into the frames, using the office ones as an example. I experimented with words and letters and the next day the new stamps were ready.

The engineer was impressed and delighted and offered to send me to Moscow to study and then rejoin him in the factory. That was a very appealing offer, but I did have a condition: I wanted to bring my girlfriend from Rozhysche to Russia to stay with me.

With his help I got my I.D. card back, money to cover expenses, and a signed permit to leave and return to Russia. I would go to Rozhysche, get Genia and then go to Moscow to study.

Genia's brother was allowed to join me and so we set out on our journey.

## Moscow

Moscow is on the way to Rozhysche. It was there that I rode on an underground train for the first time in my life.

We had no relatives, friends or any other people to stay with in Moscow so we spent most of our time riding those trains and as long as we didn't leave the underground we could use the same ticket.

Many homeless people roamed the streets. At night, ropes were stretched from building to building and the homeless hung their arms over the ropes and slept.

While staying in Moscow I encountered two incidents very typical to this country.

One day, while walking in the street I was approached by a Russian policeman. He asked for my I.D. and any other documents I had. Then he took me to the police station. I had no fear, since my documents were legal and I had a signed permit to move all over Russia.

At the station, I was given a very "educational" interrogation. At first, the policeman asked where I came from. I told him I came from Łódź and emphasized I was sent by the factory. That didn't interest him.

He wanted to know how many rooms were in my home in Łódź. When he heard about the size of the apartment my family lived in, he commented: "You were middle class family, which means you belonged to the Bonds party." This was the Jewish labor party in Łódź. Realizing where the question was leading, I replied innocently: "No, my mom threatened us kids that if any of us joined a political activity we wouldn't be allowed to live at home."

When he couldn't find any evidence that I belonged to a political party, and couldn't blame me with any illegal issue, and therefore wasn't a candidate to be sent to Siberia, he released me.

With harmless questions, the authorities could find a reason to convict anybody to forced labor. This was very common in communist Russia at that time.

The other incident still brings tears to my eyes.

Wherever we were, we could always spot a Jew—they weren't hard to recognize.

On one of my underground trips, I met a Jew. After we exchanged the regular information such as "from where to where", the fellow told me a story directly from faraway, cold Siberia.

He had been a prisoner in Siberia and had been released. Before his release one of the Russian inmates gave him a letter addressed to that inmate's wife in Moscow and asked him to drop the letter into a mailbox in Moscow, to avoid censorship.

Also, he didn't want to jeopardize the man's freedom by sending him to visit the wife of a convict.

The startling part of the story was the reason for that inmate's arrest.

He used to own a liquor store in Moscow. One night his friend came into the store and bought liquor for a party. Later that night he came back for more alcohol. It was after hours and illegal to sell alcohol. After some begging, the storeowner sold some more. The third time, he refused. His friend, heavily drunk, yelled "You'll regret this refusal".

Not too long after the incident, the inmate was accused of selling liquor after hours and sent to Siberia. Somebody snitched.

Every time his release date was approaching, he was accused of some felony and his sentence was prolonged. He realized that he would never be released.

The letter to his wife released her to remarry and go on with her life.

A story from Siberia.

## Back to Rozhysche

We continued our journey, supporting ourselves by painting signs, repairing watches, cutting wood, whatever we could do.

On April 1940 we arrived back at Rozhysche and I joined Genia.

Mr. Berger refused to host an unmarried couple in his home so in Ukraine, torn apart from our beloved families and having no idea what the future held for us, Genia and I got married. It was a double wedding—Tsesha and Genia's brother got married too.

After the wedding, Henia Torchenuke invited us to spend a honeymoon at her house and in spite of the hard times and shortage of food we had a wonderful time. Henia treated us as if we were her own children.

We were speechless then and I am speechless now. There are no words to describe our gratitude.

It was time to go back to Moscow to study, but the roads to Russia were closed. Nobody could travel from Ukraine to Russia. I had to write my kind engineer from the factory, and inform him about my situation.

Unfortunately I couldn't return to the factory.

## Genia in Rozhysche

*While in Rozhysche we accepted any job in order to make money.*

*For a while David and my brother and I sold ice cream on the street. This was actually a very good job. Even though we were three people, each of us had a good income.*

*After a while I was employed by a restaurant as a dishwasher and soon was promoted to a waitress position. To be a waitress in Ukraine in those days was a very good income job.*

*Most of the customers were army officers, often drunk and loaded with money. They ate well, drank a lot, and most of all, tipped well.*

*Still, the waiters used the "Drinking factor" to their advantage.*

*This is how it worked:*

*On the bill after a meal, the waiter would write the date, for example Oct. 8th 1940, in a column like this:*

*8*
*10*
*40*

*Then he would write the number of dishes, and the price of each dish, and the total:*

*2 number of dishes*
*3 price per dish*
*6 price of both dishes*

*Next he would write the number of bottles of wine, price per bottle, and the total:*

*3 bottles of wine*
*2.5 price per bottle*
*7.5 price of all three bottles*

*Lastly, he would add up the column of numbers, and add the tax:*

*82 (which included the date)*
*7 taxes*
-----
*90.0 The Bill.*

*On top of this, the officers added a tip.*

*One of the waiters told me one night that he already made a month's salary.*

*Tsesha, my sister in law, was a wonderful girl with a heart of gold.*

*We were very good friends until the end of the war. She used to bake fresh rolls and bring them to David and me. Coaxing us to eat them. "Eat, eat" she would say. " I know you are used to good food." After the war she left my brother and discontinued our relationship. She didn't want to have any connection to my brother.*

*Dear, dear Tsesha, I miss you. I hope life is good to you, wherever you are.*

## Scenes of War, 1941

In 1941, the Germans advanced towards Ukraine. Many buildings were burning, stores were being looted. We had to flee Rozhysche.

We boarded a train, some of the last ones to leave our area. Twenty four hours passed and the train didn't move. Impatient people left the cars, started to walk and after a while got tired and came back.

In our car was a large family—brothers, their wives and kids, and a baby. Eventually, they ran out of diapers and the mother got off the train to look for more. As she left, the train started to move. The whole large family panicked, cries and yells filled the car, but nobody dared to leave.

The story has a happy ending:

The manager of the train station was the last to leave. He drove off in a locomotive and took the mother with him and at the next stop the family was reuinted.

(After the war I met the couple in Israel. They lived in Natanya, and ran a very prosperous company, growing and selling flowers.)

On our way to Russia the German airplanes shot at the train but luckily, the train didn't stop.

The first sight upon arriving in Russia was a young shepherd girl. She poked at her goats and called them "jidka" (Jew), probably because they had little beards.

We were distributed among the people of a village (*kolkhoz* in Russian).

Most of the people were kind hearted—if one entered a home while the family was eating, one was invited to share the food no matter how little there was.

Genia and I lived with a family of three: a mother, a son and a father in law. The husband had been drafted.

Soon we were introduced to habits and ways of life foreign to us.

In the kolkhoz, men and women took baths together. The mother in this family was originally from Leningrad and she was not used to the local customs and therefore refused to take baths together with her father in law. He was mocked for this by his friends.

To get back at her, he didn't support the family. This created hardship on the woman because with her husband away in the army, there was no other adult man in the family and her child was sick.

The grandfather in this family was a very experienced fisherman. He knew the good spots along the river where fish were concentrated and used to mark the good spots with pegs, to which he tied his nets. In the evening, he went from one spot to another and collected the day's catch.

I told the little grandson to follow his grandfather and learn were the good spots were. Then in midday, the boy and I went to those spots and collected part of the caught fish, always leaving some. By the evening more fish were caught in the nets so that the grandfather didn't notice. Everybody had enough food.

The Russian villagers stored fresh grass in large pits to have feed for the animals in winter. The stored grass was called *selyez.*

The procedure was simple: The farmers dug pits, filled them with fresh grass and covered them. The cold kept the grass fresh. When winter arrived and animals could not graze in the fields, the pits were uncovered and the stored grass was pulled out and fed to the animals.

But not all soil was fit for this kind of storage—fertile soil caused the grass to rot, and the soil in our village was fertile. Still, Moscow issued an order to dig pits for selyez. All the refugees were under army command so we were ordered to dig.

For people not used to physical labor, it was a very hard task. But this was our ticket to survival and we didn't complain.

An old man from the village asked us why we were digging. We replied that we were digging pits for selyez. He laughed "Selyez will not be here!" Our angry commander shooed him away and ordered us to continue with our work. Actually, he knew the old man was right. Still, he carried out the order from Moscow.

Why would the commander carry out a task that he knew would probably fail? The answer—fear. He was afraid to disobey an order from above, or to tell his superiors they were wrong. Fear was the driving force in every action. As a result, plans failed, orders produced no results and no products.

That incident, the first in many events of that nature that I encountered during my stay in Russia explained why in spite of the massive human and natural resources, Russia couldn't recover from its failing economy.

The end of the story is obvious: The grass rotted and was discarded.

In another example, winter was approaching and we had to collect potatoes for storage. We had to dig up the potatoes, load them on wagons, and get the wagons to the storage spot called *pagrev.*

It was extremely important not to include damaged potatoes with good ones, since the damaged ones could infect the whole crop, and so destroy the winter food supply.

As usual, an order came from Moscow to collect potatoes. This time they added a deadline.

There weren't enough wagons to create an uninterrupted work line, so after first load of potatoes was transferred and stored safely on time, we had to wait for the wagons to come back. This created a delay and because now the project was not proceeding according to schedule, the commander didn't wait for the wagons to arrive and ordered us to dig out more potatoes.

We had to cover the recently dug potatoes with sacks and wait over night for the wagons. The cold night was not kind to our potatoes and many got damaged. Next day the potatoes were loaded, damaged as well as good, and stored with the first load of potatoes.

When winter came and the potatoes were uncovered, most of them were infected and damaged.

Our wives were sent to the storage site to separate the good potatoes from the bad ones. A huge snowstorm blocked the way back to the village and with no other food our trapped wives ate all the good potatoes.

Again, fearing punishment for not meeting the expected deadline, the project failed.

The villagers cultivated national fields, but each home had a small private patch of land next to it on which the owners could grow vegetables for private use.

Because the rest of the potatoes were consumed by our hungry wives, each household was required to donate two buckets of potatoes to be planted for the next year's crop.

Up to this point we had been working in fields, living with families in the villages. But now we refugees were drafted to defend a town called Saratov which had become a battle front. I had to leave Genia behind.

There were villages in Russia inhabited for many years by Germans. One such village, Mor, was near Saratov. The German residents of that village had been ordered by the Russians to evacuate, but leave their animals for use by the Russian army.

When we entered the village we saw many wolves gathered around the barns. When we got inside the barns, we saw why—the German residents had locked the animals in the barns without food so that they would die and be of no use to the Russian army.

The houses in the village were fit very well for winter. 60cm thick walls kept the heat in and the cold out.

We were fifteen soldiers to a house and we dug tunnels to our tanks to avoid having to walk in the cold. We took turns cleaning and procuring food. I befriended a French soldier, one of the fifteen in our house. Both of us knew that food would be a problem so we loosened a brick in the wall and hid pieces of dried bread. Nobody could tell where the 'treasure' was.

We were often summoned by the sound of a bugle and lined up in rows. Approximately 100 soldiers at a time were selected in random, loaded on trucks and left to the front line.

## Genia left behind

*When the men were drafted the women stayed behind.*

*We were not ready for the Russian winter. We couldn't work wearing only light coats that we brought from Poland. Because we couldn't work, our food rations were small and we depended on the hosting families.*

*I was assigned to a woman who was not very kind, nor was her daughter.*

*The woman, her daughter, and her mother milked their cows and made butter and sour cream. Buckets of wonderful white stuff were lined up in the house, in front of me. Not only wasn't I offered any, but the daughter used to eat from the buckets in front of me and smirk.*

*I decided to join David in the front line.*

*I traded food stamps for a jar of butter and a jar of honey. I packed a small backpack with my few belongings and started my journey, walking by foot in the snow with no clue what direction to take. Hours passed, the wind blowing in my face, the snow stretching in front of me. No people, no houses, no trees.*

*After hours of marching, I finally saw a man riding on a horse. I asked for directions to Mor. Following his directions, I finally came upon villages. At night I would knock at a door of a house (or a hut, to be more precise) asking to spend the night. The villagers were very kind. They let me in and usually also fed me.*

*After a few days, I arrived at Mor.*

*Very tired, half starving and almost frozen, I entered the headquarters office. Before I even opened my mouth, the secretary asked: "Are you Genia?"*

*My jaw dropped. "How do you know?"*

*"Your husband talks so much about you that it would be impossible NOT to recognize you."*

*When I met David I wanted to surprise him with the treats I had, I couldn't find the butter and the honey. Somewhere, somebody looked through my backpack while I was sleeping!*

*The food shortage was such a big problem that I had to turn around and go back to the village I came from. On my way back, a pregnant woman joined me. She had been released from prison due to her advanced pregnancy. She would knock on every door to ask for food. I waited for her in the distance, embarrassed. Each night I joined her to sleep inside a warm hut.*

*One night we entered a hut. The owner, an old woman, arranged a sleeping area on the floor for the 'released prisoner', and told me to climb up on top of the fireplace, the most desired place in the hut to sleep. Even though I didn't ask for food, she made cheese stuffed crapes and brought them up to me.*

*I will never forget such a moment of grace.*

## How one gets rid of a "headache"

One day, working in the tunnel we had dug to get to our tanks, I felt sick but didn't pay attention. In the morning I couldn't move. The doctor was summoned. It turned out that my stay in the tunnel resulted in pneumonia.

I was sent to a hospital, since pneumonia was a serious illness.

Due to the shortage of beds, the hospital management decided to release a few soldiers who were still in the recovery process. Although I was still in need of medical attention, I was loaded onto an army truck along with thirteen other sick soldiers to be sent back to our respective villages.

On the way, the driver let villagers climb up the truck with their produce and other products. They were headed to a town market to sell their goods.

After we crossed the Volga, we arrived at a small town. The driver took a break and told us to leave our stuff on the truck and go get some tea and stretch our legs, while he filled the truck with gasoline.

All of us, including the villagers, left the truck and went to have some tea and breathe fresh air.

Two hours later, we realized that the driver had gone off with all our belongings and the villagers' goods. He left us without food, clothes, or any solution.

Every village had a military headquarters and the commander in charge was responsible for everything that was going on in his area. The commander of that area now had a problem, and he needed to get rid of us as soon as possible.

To earn our trust he behaved in a sly manner: In our presence, he ordered one of his men to make a list of all the soldiers that were in our group and then go to supplies and bring for each of us bread, salami, and cigarettes. He also gave us train tickets.

He ordered his man to follow us to the train and make sure we all embarked on it.

We were very pleased.

The train drove to the next station and stopped. We were told by that station's manager to get off since it was the train's last stop. The stations were far enough from each other that we couldn't walk back in our condition.

We learned a bitter lesson. The commander knew that there was only one more stop, but needing to get rid of his "headache" (thirteen sick soldiers), he had conned us into leaving on the train.

The soldier in charge of our group got scared. He was worried that he would be punished for what had happened, so he ran away.

We were left, confused and helpless. Suddenly somebody yelled: "Kdo kuda" (*Everybody to himself*).

We scattered, each to his fate.

It was winter in Russia.

Snow and gray sky. It was dark and I was alone. I tried to follow footsteps in the snow but it was too dark—I could not see anything. I was reduced to using my sense of touch. Finally I felt walls. I continued to feel the walls until I found a doorknob.

When I opened the door it turned out I was lucky to enter the headquarters office of that kolkhoz.

Nobody was inside so I set down and waited. After a while, two women came in. I explained my situation and one of them gave me a note to the nearest family house, permitting me to sleep there.

I left the office, and started walking in the snowstorm. Again, I felt walls, then a doorknob, but when I opened the door I stepped into the same office. It was very late, too dark and I was too tired to go out again. I moved a table closer to the fireplace and fell asleep on it.

The following day I couldn't open the door. I was snowed in. I had to wait until somebody shoveled the snow away.

The snow was removed only enough to clear a path to the water well.

When I finally came out and inquired how I could get to my destination, I was told that a tractor was living the village towards the neighboring village. I couldn't ride the tractor but I could follow it. My shoes were not adequate for walking that distance in the snow, so I put my gloves on my feet and ran after the tractor to the next kolkhoz.

A few adventures later I arrived at "my" kolkhoz.

When I arrived, my physical condition was so bad, I couldn't breathe right and I couldn't sleep in a bed. I slept on the floor for a few nights.

## Genia Tells

*When David returned from the hospital he was in a very bad physical condition. I didn't recognize him. As soon as he arrived he fell asleep.*

*I went to buy butter, milk and bread.*

*The next day, the healing process started. The rest and the good food helped. After a short time he was himself again.*

*When my landlady saw him healthy she was shocked. "I thought your husband is an old man", she said.*

*She was also very upset since I didn't buy the dairy products from her.*

*I felt a slight satisfaction thinking about my small "revenge".*

*When David got well, we moved to another home.*

## Foul ups and Beating the system

Food was supplied according to production and since I had worked all the previous summer I was owed a lot of bread.

In those days in Russia bread was a very important source of nutrition. We could survive on bread and tea. Therefore, bread served as salary. People saved, stole and traded bread.

When I came to the storehouse and asked for my share of bread, the lady in charge laughed. "He feels like bread!" she mocked me. It turned out that the kolkhoz received little bread that year.

I turned to other sources of income. I repaired watches and clocks, sewed clothes, and whatever I could put my hands on. The exchange was food and other necessary items.

One day I repaired a grandfather clock which had been inactive for many years. A few days after the repair, the owner came running, alarmed. The clock chimed thirteen times.

Weeks passed. One day I was summoned to the Commanders office. He informed me that he was sending me to a bookkeeping class. They needed a bookkeeper in the tractors department. One of the laws at that time entitled a person to refuse to work if one didn't get one's bread portion, so I refused to go.

I returned to the house where I was staying and continued to accept all kinds of odd jobs. Finally the commander gave in. I got my bread and went to the nearby village were the class was being held.

While the disagreement with the commander was going on, the class was going on too. By the time I arrived the class was over, but the instructor tested me anyway. It turned out that I actually knew the material enough to qualify as a bookkeeper. I was sent to the bookkeeping manager and got my first assignment.

My first assignment was to send him a report every five days with information about the quantities of diesel used in our village. When I returned to the village, I couldn't find any diesel in the barrels. They were all empty. Five days passed and I still had no idea how the diesel was used.

The commander had no idea either. He sent me to the man in charge of the vehicles. Mr. "In Charge" had lost one eye in combat and had been sent to the rear front. He knew how to beat the system.

I explained my problem.

“Do you want to live?” he asked.

“Of course” I said.

“O.K. Then. Do as I say”

He dictated a report: “We sent two tractors to the right field but it was too muddy, then we sent the tractors to the left field, it was too dry. We also borrowed a combine machine from the neighboring village and had to return it, using our fuel.”

I almost laughed. Those were such clear lies.

“I am not signing such a report”, I protested.

“Nobody asks you to sign. You write, and I sign.” replied the one eyed veteran. He didn’t know to write. That was my job.

I was curious: “So where is the diesel?”

“Did you expect the village to stay in the dark?”

The second project was even more intriguing.

Bread was rationed to the kolkhoz according to a simple formula: The authorities calculated how much wheat a fertile field would produce, then calculated how much bread could be produced from that crop.

From that calculated yield, thirty percent would be sent to the military and the remaining seventy percent went to the village.

I measured how many fertile hectares of land belonged to the village so we could calculate our bread allotment, but my measurements didn’t match those of the year before. According to my measurements, the village actually had 100 hectare less than the number reported the preceding year. The commander didn’t believe me and sent another man to the fields for a second opinion. His measurements matched mine.

When I checked in the neighboring village’s archives, I found out that somebody indeed made a mistake the year before and reported 100 hectare more.

The fact explained why the village didn’t receive enough bread that year:

Since on paper the kolkhoz had hundred hectare of fertile land more than in reality, the predicted yield was artificially inflated. Because the thirty percent sent to the military was calculated from that inflated number, the remainder wasn't a true seventy percent, and the village received quite a bit less than it should have.

The commander was a new appointee and the people that had created the mess were long gone. He was very frightened because guilty or not, he knew that if the facts leaked out he would pay the price. Since I was the only one who knew about the foul-up he had to get rid of me.

At home I told Genia, "I am not going to stay here too long."

While having my physical in the clinic I overheard the commander comment to one of his men, "We have to get rid of him."

And they did.

I was sent to a far away camp, where the army was experimenting with Katyusha rocket launchers.

## Genia moves again

*When David was sent away I was moved to another family, a grandmother, her daughter and a grandson. The women were not very generous and I was hungry most of the time.*

*One day the boy was having a hard time with his homework so I worked with him on his problems. When mother and grandma realized they had a tutor in residence, they changed their ways.*

*From that day on I ate with the family and grandma knitted gloves and slippers for me.*

*When I left my home in Łódź, I had taken with me a white bed sheet and a white pillowcase. Wherever I went I had them with me, white and crisp. The grandma, very impressed, used to invite neighbors to see my bed.*

## Survival

Although my new destination [from June 1943 to June 1945 in Syzran, Russia] was classified and very remote, not being a soldier or a local, I was not given a secretive job: my partner and I were assigned to guard the melon fields. The biggest problem was the animals grazing in the melon fields. We shot them, using salt bullets which caused enough burning sensation to keep them away.

My partner, Makoovin Vaslenovitz, came from a very backward place. When he first saw a train he ran away frightened. Since that day he was the butt of jokes when trains were mentioned.

On our way to the supply point, we used to stop at a basement where bees were kept during the winter. An old guard took care of them. One day the old man gave us two small bowls full with honey, and he presented a challenge: If we could eat the honey without using bread, he promised to give us honey every day. We tried. But eventually we used up the bread ration for the whole week. He showed us how we could do it. He took a spoonful of honey and then sipped water, again honey and then water. We did the same and finished two bowls of honey without bread. But that was the last time we got honey from him.

After melon season was over we joined a group of twenty men, most of them locals. Our quarters were located near the train station and we worked for the army in non-secretive jobs.

Daily survival was a struggle. Food shortages, personnel shortages, political pressure and homelessness all took their toll. Also, it was not easy to work next to locals because they received food and supplies from home, while we suffered from hunger.

I recognized a fellow who fled Ukraine the same time as I did. His name was Shleserenko. We became buddies and with him by my side I was able to survive that hard period.

We depended on the army for food. We received dry supplies and food stamps to buy soup once a day, which was the only hot meal we got.

Two guys used to go every evening with our food stamps and buy the soup from a restaurant kitchen. It was very diluted and did not satisfy our hunger.

I hatched a plan. I told Shleserenko to pretend not to know me, start to complain about the diluted soup and suggest we needed new people to bring the soup from the restaurant and told me to then mention me as a candidate.

He followed my instructions. The plan worked. I was selected to be the new soup carrier and as a helper I chose Shlesersnko.

That evening, before we left to the restaurant I hid a half litter bottle of vodka under my coat. Arriving at the restaurant I went to the kitchen's back door. When the cook answered the knocking, I presented him with the food stamps and slipped the vodka into his hands. This time the cook filled the pot with good quality soup. At my request he also added an extra pot with thick ingredients such as meat, vegetables and beans.

We returned to the camp carrying two treasures. There are no words to describe the joyous welcome we received.

That evening, I invited Shleserenko to join me on a trip to the restaurant. He was confused. Since we already used all our food stamps and we didn't have money, why would we go back to the restaurant? I showed him that I had saved a few stamps for our use—we had enough for two good meals.

We went to the restaurant and celebrated!

From that day on, we brought those wonderful pots with their amazing contents every evening. I was named "Boyeboy Faren". In loose translation: "A jolly good fellow".

Even though now we ate well we needed money or its equal to use for trading. Without local families to support us and very little pay, we needed extra sources of income.

Since most of the local men had been drafted, the women left behind needed help, especially cutting wood for the fireplaces and the cooking ovens.

I overheard one of the secretaries at the train station office talking about her hardship and I offered my help. I asked Shleserenko to join me and we earned some money cutting wood for her fireplace.

Thereafter, I would look into the yards in the village. If I noticed a pile of wood waiting to be chopped, I offered our services.

Shleserenko was so grateful that he didn't let me work. Being a large, strong man, he could manage the work by himself. It became a routine: I found the jobs and he carried them out.

We became very good friends and took care of each other. Shleserenko was feared by everybody and so protected me. And when he got sick and was hospitalized I visited him daily, bringing good food and slowly nurturing him back to health.

## Genia joins the group

In honor of May 1st, the commander prepared a feast with wines, liquor and ample food. VIPs were coming. But the Russians, the drunkards, consumed everything before the arrival of the important guests.

Embarrassed, the commander had to choose a new man to put in charge of food and supplies: Starshina in Russian. I was known as a hard worker, non-drinker and not a woman chaser. Those were excellent qualities for the job.

He knew he could trust me.

When he offered me the job I agreed with an "If".

"If?", laughed the commander. "This is an order."

I knew my rights. As long as I did my job well I didn't have to accept a new job.

"What is the condition?" He was curious.

"I want to transfer my wife to our camp." I said.

"There is no room for a woman here."

"Well, we have a nurse. We can have two."

He thought for a while and I got permission to bring my wife.

## ***Genia Tells***

*While David was away, I befriended all the other women refugees. We created a very strong bond and became a tight group, but when David arrived to take me away I was out of my mind with joy.*

*The hunger, the cold and the helplessness all were going to be memories of the past.*

*I packed my stuff and loaded it onto a sled that David had made. All my friends stood next to us and cried as we departed. We knew there was a very slim chance we would ever meet again.*

*I left the Kolchoz with mixed feelings. On one hand, I felt a huge relief. On the other hand, sadness flooded my heart.*

*I knew that another chapter of my life just came to an end.*

## Genia Joins the Camp (cont.)

Genia very quickly became part of our group.

She worked with me. Her duty was to dispense the daily bread portions and other supplies for each day. At the end of a workday, all the workers lined up in front of a serving window and Genia gave out the bread portions according to the quantity of cut wood each worker produced.

Genia, with her turquoise almond shaped eyes, her chestnut hair, her perfect shaped figure and manners of a delicate princess, was loved by everyone.

Since there were no women around, the men used to swear and curse. But if somebody happened to swear in her presence he was quickly hushed up by everybody else.

"Quiet", they would say. "Genitchka is listening."

This wonderful attitude was mutual. Genia did her best to help.

We had a very hard worker with the reputation for large quota achievements. One day he didn't meet his usual production. Nevertheless, knowing he had a wife and a child to provide for Genia gave him his usual bread portion.

He protested: "I didn't meet the usual quota"

"To me", said Genia, "you are always a *malazetsz* (high achiever).

Editor's Note:

My mom lived among Russian women. Most of them were kind and very superstitious.

Once when my dad was away buying supplies for the camp, she had a strange dream. She told the dream to an old Russian woman. That woman's interpretation was that my dad had been robbed and she even told my mom how many items had been stolen.

When my dad returned with a "long face" my mom immediately told him how many items were stolen and how much money was gone.

The facts were correct.

## Spying Snitching and Saving

I had duties in addition to being in charge of food and supplies.

As the war continued, more and more refuges filled the country. They were political refuges, people that managed to escape from hell, deserters and so on. In every populated area the government had "concentration spots". When people without I.D. cards were caught, they were brought to those points.

Once in a while I went to a spot like that and recruited people to work at our camp. I was choosing them according to our needs. If we needed tailors I was looking for tailors. If we needed carpenters, carpenters were the lucky ones. When all the professionals were recruited, I chose people with no qualifications to dig pits, chop wood etc.

I tried to save as many Jews as I could. I could always recognize a Jew.

One day I identified a young boy as a Jew. To my question about his qualifications he said he used to be an assistant to a tailor. He promised he could sew anything needed. He also had a friend with him. I suggested to him to claim to be a tailor too. As we were looking for tailors I took them to our camp. The whole time we stayed in the camp those two boys didn't forget I saved their lives.

They showed their appreciation in many ways. One particular episode is a nice example:

A forest ranger told me one day that soon he would have a fox fur for Genia. While on duty, he noticed a fox around the chicken coup. Not very long after, he caught the fox and the two "tailors" sewed a fur coat for Genia.

In wartime, while shortages of everything were a part of life, Genia was wearing a new, beautiful custom made fox fur coat.

Editor's Note:

My dad told me about one of the times when he hired a Jew at one of the "concentration spots". The man claimed he had escaped a concentration camp. His story was amazing.

Not too long after they arrived at the camp. He and a few other men were assigned the task of shoveling bodies into the oven. While shoveling bodies, they noticed that a few of the bodies were not as thin and sick looking as the rest.

After some discussion they concluded that those were the bodies of the men that preceded them at the same job, and were killed to keep them from telling what was going on. That was the reason the bodies were in better condition. They were killed early, and didn't have time to lose weight.

They knew they had to escape.

"What did we have to lose?" said the man. "They would have killed us anyway."

How they escaped, he didn't reveal.

He also didn't know the fate of the others. After the escape it was each to his fate.

He survived and ended up in Russia.

When my dad was away getting stuff for the camp, my mom got sick with malaria. Not much could be done but wait. Shleserenko was worried sick. He sat next to her bed day and night, changing wet towels on her forehead to reduce the fever.

Once in a while he listened to her breathing to make sure she was still alive.

He was crying all that time.

"What am I going to tell David if something happens?" he wept.

My mom was delirious for a long time. When the doctor thought it was the turning point night, Shlesernko cried and prayed, cried and prayed until the fever broke and my mom started to get better.

Every so often, workers were blamed for being disloyal to the country. They were quickly sentenced and sent to Siberia.

One of my duties was to supply them with clothes and some other necessary things. When I received an order to prepare a package of clothes, I knew somebody was going to be tried for treason.

Once a very honest working fellow was tried for a very ridiculous reason, but at the time it was serious. Somebody claimed hearing him yell at his friend: "U tee bia durnaia bashka kak otoverishka Stalina." Translation: "You have a stupid head like comrade Stalin."

The fellow was sentenced to hard work in Siberia, and I was ordered to prepare his going away package.

This fellow's partner at work, a Jew and a very honest guy, testified against his friend. After the trial, I asked him why he did it since he knew the fellow was innocent.

He answered, "David, I was interrogated in such a way that if I claimed he was innocent it would have made me the guilty one."

"I don't understand." I said.

"How lucky you are."

Not for long. Eventually, I was summoned to the secret police office.

The local secret police commander selected me to be his snitch. My code name was Vasili, *the happy one*. He was very direct. In his opinion, since I knew all the workers and they trusted me, I could easily find spies and traitors.

My duty was to report everything I heard and sign my code name. When I left the office I knew my life was not going to be easy. I definitely was not going to blame innocent people.

Because I wasn't discovering any spies and traitors I was nudged a little further—I was ordered to interview suspects.

For example a Jewish refugee arrived from the "concentration spot". He told us that he escaped from the Nazis. He was suspected to be a Nazi in disguise. I was in charge of his interrogation. I knew he already submitted his life story. His answers to my interrogation had to match his life story. I couldn't be frank with him and tell him to say what he had written in his report so I could report the same, since we never knew who was a snitch. He might have been sent to check me out. So, I started with an innocent conversation and along the way asked him to tell me what he wrote in his report about his life. Then I submitted a report with that information as questions and answers, knowing those facts would match his report.

The head of the secret police in our area didn't like my inactivity. He called me to his office and was very blunt: "You know everybody here, you chat with the guys, listen to their conversations, they trust you and don't hide their opinions from you. It's impossible you haven't heard or seen something pointing towards treason or disloyalty to the country. There are many spies among us. Still you haven't caught even a single one yet. If somebody else will find a spy, somebody you know, and you failed to do it first you'll be considered a collaborator."

I was worried. I knew I had to find a way to get out of there.

The way out was carefully planned and executed.

The first stage was finding a job for Genia in town away from the camp. She moved away.

The second stage was conditioning the state of mind of my commander.

The bookkeeper in the Commander's office (Alex) was a nice man, but a drunkard like most others. On one winter night, a month prior my scary interview, I found him lying in the street, very drunk. I knew that left there he would freeze to death.

I carried him on my back to his living quarters, covered him, put his shoes under his head, and asked his roommates to keep quiet and let him sleep.

When he woke up in the morning and found out what happened he wept. Since then, he became a very good friend of mine.

As he was not a Jew and was a regular in the main office, I could use his help without raising suspicion.

At that time the camp couldn't supply the quota of cut wood. The commander was very worried, as he could be sent to Siberia.

I asked Alex to chat with the commander and inject the suggestion to send me to the forest. I went over with him what to say: "David will make sure the quota will be met, and, anyway, why do you need a Jew among us?"

Alex carried out his part of the plan.

The third stage was the most critical one.

I asked a permission to go and visit my wife in town. The commander smiled, approving a twenty four hour leave.

The next day I took a backpack and went to the train station. I waited until the train left and turned around back to the camp. Everybody thought that I was on my way to town.

On my way back I saw a wagon collecting wheat from the villagers. That year the kolchoz didn't produce enough wheat to send to the government. The commander, fearing punishment, was collecting donations from the villagers' private crops.

He was very angry and scared to see me.

I could snitch if I wanted.

At that point he had to get rid of me. I was sent to the forest to chop wood.

The next morning I informed the head of the secret police about my transfer.

And so my job as an informer came to an end.

Cutting wood was my last job in Russia. I stayed in the forest until the end of the war.

In the beginning of 1946, when I came back to the camp to be released and paid, the commander offered me to stay and work with him. He promised to send me to Moscow to study. But I wanted to find my family. He understood that.

Then I went to the secret police office to be formally released from my duty as an informer. To my great disappointment I was assigned to look for spies on the train to Poland.

Pretending to be sick, I assigned somebody else to replace me on the train. I was "sick" all the way to Poland. I returned to Łódź on June 25, 1946.

## Israel 1965

### Twenty years later, Tel Aviv

My wife and my older daughter were sitting in a tailor's parlor waiting for their dresses to be finished, chatting with the other women.

Anytime a group gathered, the subjects of conversation were always the same: The past in Europe, the war period, and the immigration to Israel.

One of the women started to converse with my wife. "Where are you from?"

"I am from Łódź." said my wife.

The woman, excited, said, "I know Łódź is big but maybe you know somebody by the name of David Krimalowsky?"

"Yes" said my wife. "He is my husband!"

"Do you know if he stayed a short time in Rozhysche?"

"Yes, and I was there too. And who are you?" she asked the woman.

"I am Shula, Torchenuk's little girl."

Genia and Shula fell into each other's arms crying and laughing.

Everybody present wept.

The following day we visited Shula and her family. Henia and Pnina survived the war. Shoshana, Hadassa and her family and Dov perished in the Holocaust. Bat-Zion lived in the kibbutz Beith Hashita. Henia lived there too.

We renewed our tight bond with Henia, Pnina-le, her husband Baruch and with Shula and her husband Alex. Alex. The kind Alex.

Warmth, love and kindness engulfed Genia and me.

Out of the sadness and darkness of our endeavors a beam of light carrying love, courage, determination, perseverance and hope, is gleaming at us. I recognize the light: I know it. It's the Human Spirit.

David Krimalowsky

June 21st 1994

Ramat Gan, Israel

## Biographies

David Krimalowsky (1910-2000) was born in Łódź, Poland, the youngest of five children.

For a few years life was good. His father Anshel was a prosperous merchant and was respected by his peers. However when on a business trip to Germany, he contracted typhus and upon returning home got very sick and died. His entire family was taken to a hospital and was kept in isolation until it was proven that they had not contracted the disease.

The family owned a grocery store located under their apartment and to avoid looting while they were in the hospital, they put a sign on the store door reading "Typhus". However, the warning didn't work and when the family came back home all the goods were gone.

The family never recovered from that loss. David's mother operated a smaller grocery store at the same location but the good years were over.

His brother Itsak, ten years his senior, got married and moved to Israel to avoid being drafted by the Polish army.

Velvle (Ze'ev), David's second brother got married, had a son and stayed close to the family.

Since money was scarce, David and his two sisters, Lea and Ruza, had to go to work at an early age.

So after graduating from elementary school, David got a job designing underwear at a Jewish-owned factory.

Hungry for knowledge, he continued to study and improve in many areas. He and a few friends hired a college student to teach them mathematics, physics and other science subjects. They also read classic books and listened to fine music.

David joined a group of young Jewish boys and girls that met in the evenings, discussed current affairs, and played chess.

They founded a nonprofessional acting company and were lucky to attract a famous professional director and a well known choreographer who helped them to produce plays on stage. David was very talented: he was an actor, a dancer, sang well and was also a stand-up comedian and a Master of Ceremonies. In addition to these skills he was an accomplished photographer and built a photo developing lab in his home.

These young Jewish boys and girls used to meet in the home of friends (three boys and two girls) whose parents were dead. The siblings continued to live together, the boys working and the girls running the household. These siblings were Genia's cousins.

It was a very welcoming home, without the strictness of parents.

Throughout his life, David was very motivated and gifted. He wrote poems and short stories, painted, had a warm and beautiful singing voice and an immense desire to learn. He could read, speak and write Hebrew, Yiddish, Polish, Russian, and German. When he was over eighty years old he took up the study of English.

Two of David's strongest qualities were his persistence, and his solution oriented thinking.

He and Genia moved to Israel after the war, had two daughters and lived there until their passing.

Genia Koenigsberg (1915-1997) was born in a small town in Poland named Socoli. She was the youngest of six children. Her father Avraham died of tuberculosis when she was a very little girl.

Her older brother Gedalia was sent to his grandparents in Łódź to study in a yeshiva but he suffered from hunger and harsh treatment. While still quite young, he ran away from the yeshiva to Russia and joined the communists, where he quickly ascended to leadership positions. One day the letters to him started coming back with the word "unknown" printed on them. The family lost contact and never heard from him again.

Leon, the second brother, was also a rebel. He escaped from Poland and went to America. For many years the family didn't hear from him and he was presumed dead.

Meanwhile, Genia's mother (Pearl) decided to move back to her hometown of Łódź to rejoin her family. One day a letter arrived from Leon. He had done well financially and the letter contained a huge sum of money. But Pearl's joy was short lived. Her sister insisted on handling the money, and Pearl never saw it again.

Thereafter, the family suffered. Even though the two remaining brothers Mendel and Herschel, and Genia's older sister Ruza worked, they never had the future they were so looking forward to.

While still in elementary school Genia contributed to the family finances by tutoring other children.

When Genia finished school, she was awarded a scholarship to a famous Jewish high school for girls in Łódź.  She never graduated from this school, presumably because of the war.

Genia used to visit her cousins and there she met David. They became a couple and were popular and loved.  Genia was a known beauty. She was also a wise woman and well educated in social etiquette. The staff at the retirement home where Genia spent her final days referred to her as “The Princess”.

"Yiddishe Theatre-Studio" Łódź – 1935
David Krimalowsky (seated row, far right)
Genia's cousin (seated row, second from left). David and Genia met in his house.
Shlomo Yankelevitch (second row, far left). David and Shlomo were friends until their deaths.

David and Genya in Russia

*David as a soldier in the Russian army*

www.ingramcontent.com/pod-product-compliance
Ingram Content Group UK Ltd.
Pitfield, Milton Keynes, MK11 3LW, UK
UKHW020231250726
13967UKWH00001B/309

9 781257 831241